Saints Cosmas and Damian School Library

In Memory of

Anthony Constantino

By *Faculty & Staff of SS CD. School*
1981-82

BJORN BORG

THE COOLEST ACE

Library of Congress Cataloging in Publication Data

Hahn, James.
  Björn Borg: the coolest ace.

  (Their Champions and challengers 2)
  SUMMARY: A biography of the Swedish tennis player
who in 1978 won Wimbledon for the third year in a row.
  1. Borg, Björn, 1956-   —Juvenile literature. 2. Tennis
players—Sweden—Biography—Juvenile literature. [1.
Borg, Björn, 1956-   2. Tennis players] I. Hahn, Lynn,
joint author. II. Title. III. Series.
GV994.B65H33   796.34'2'0924 [B] [92]   78-13127
  ISBN 0-88436-478-X

Published 1979. Produced by EMC Corporation
180 East Sixth Street, Saint Paul, Minnesota 55101
Printed in the United States of America
0 9 8 7 6 5 4 3 2 1

BJORN BORG

THE COOLEST ACE

BY JAMES & LYNN HAHN

EMC CORPORATION ST. PAUL, MINNESOTA

PHOTO CREDITS

Wimbledon, a London suburb, is the home of the All England Lawn Tennis and Croquet Club. Real green grass grows on the tennis courts. Lush ivy blankets the clubhouse walls. Inside, tennis players and fans are served strawberries and cream.

Every year since 1877, Wimbledon has hosted the All England Tennis Championships. Many players, fans and reporters say Wimbledon is the world championship of tennis—the most important tennis tournament in the world.

On Saturday, July 2, 1977 a slim, long-legged, blue-eyed young man from Sweden walked proudly onto Wimbledon's legendary Centre Court. Fourteen thousand fans suddenly quieted because Bjorn (pronounced Be-yorn) Borg was trying to make tennis history—trying to win Wimbledon two years in a row.

In 1976, when he was just 20 years old, Bjorn had defeated Ilie Nastase 6-4, 6-2, 9-7 to claim the trophy. Amazingly, Bjorn didn't lose a set during that tournament!

Since World War II, only four players had won Wimbledon two years in a row—Lew Hoad, Rod Laver, Roy Emerson, and John Newcombe.

Bjorn wanted his name added to that famous list. But first he had to beat the best player in the world—Jimmy Connors.

On that hot July afternoon the temperature on Centre Court steamed to 100°F. as Borg and Connors slammed the tennis ball over the net at lightning speeds.

Two different personalities challenged each other. The emotional, fiery, almost rowdy Jimmy Connors battled the cool, calm, concentrated Bjorn Borg.

Stroking a thunderous serve over the net in the first set, Bjorn's wavy, long blond hair danced. Racing wildly towards the ball, Jimmy's racket caught the bullet-like shot and launched a two-fisted backhand return.

Bjorn started too carefully and lost the first set 3-6. Some fans wondered aloud why Bjorn looked so calm and unemotional. The Iceman, as many people call Bjorn, was a model of cool concentration. His blue eyes stared at the ball so hard some fans said he was in a trance.

In the second set, Bjorn played all-out. Jimmy returned a few of Bjorn's sizzling serves. But the speedy Bjorn chased the ball and hit back tough topspin shots that Jimmy couldn't return. Bjorn won the second set 6-2.

Playing precise, almost flawless tennis, Bjorn quickly took the third set 6-1.

In the fourth set Jimmy reached way back and hit the ball with everything he had! Bjorn, looking as weak as the wilting grass on the court, lost 5-7.

Borg's style is so cool, he's called the "Iceman."

The sun seemed to be melting Bjorn and Jimmy as the match entered its third hour of play. But suddenly, Bjorn, playing sharper mentally than Jimmy, surged ahead. Serving stronger, harder, and more accurately than Jimmy, Bjorn won points. Bjorn snatched the lead with fierce forehand shots down the line and blazing backhand strokes.

Before stroking some shots, Bjorn paused to think, catching Jimmy moving the wrong way. Smashing several powerful shots deep into Jimmy's backcourt, Bjorn didn't let him have any deep angle shots.

In the fifth set, Bjorn outsmarted Jimmy, winning game, set, and match 3-6, 6-2, 6-1, 5-7, 6-4. Immediately after winning the final point, Bjorn joyfully looked up to the sky. He dropped his racket, smiled and slapped his hands on his head. He had just won Wimbledon two years in a row. Now he was the best tennis player in the world!

The fans applauded, cheered, screamed! They knew they had just watched one of the greatest tennis matches ever played.

At the awards ceremony, the Duke of Kent presented Bjorn with the gold trophy. Holding it over his head so the fans could see it, Bjorn's arms shook, they were so tired.

After 3 hours and 13 minutes of tough tennis, Bjorn looked ready to collapse. But he smiled, hugged the trophy and kissed it again and again.

"We were quite tired but happy," Mariana said at the victory dinner.

Afterwards Bjorn said it was the happiest win of his career. "It was special," he said, "to beat Jimmy at Wimbledon." He added that he had never felt so tired. Both his body and mind felt drained.

Bjorn Borg did not become the best tennis player in the world on just one July afternoon. It took him about twenty-one years. Bjorn's story began on June 6, 1956, when Rune and Margaretha Borg celebrated the birth of a baby boy—Bjorn Rune Borg.

Bjorn grew up in Sodertalje, Sweden, a manufacturing city about 40 miles from Stockholm. Many people there worked in factories, making auto parts. But Bjorn's father was a clothing salesman. His mother was a housewife.

Bjorn was an only child. He says his parents began teaching him to be a competitor when he was very young. They tacked a target onto a tree and played darts. When he lost, Bjorn cried. His parents told him to keep on playing until he won. Bjorn says he got his confidence back when he won.

In Swedish, Bjorn means bear and Borg means castle. As a young boy, friends called Bjorn Teddy Bear. Bjorn says he enjoyed playing soccer and hockey when he was growing up. When he was nine years old, he wanted to become a great hockey player. A skillful player, Bjorn played center and forward.

One night in 1965, Bjorn's father brought home a tennis racket and gave it to his son. Rune, one of Sweden's best table tennis players, had won the racket in a table tennis tournament.

Bjorn says that night was one of the turning points in his life. The next day he began hitting a tennis ball against a garage wall from morning until night.

At first, Bjorn says, it was almost impossible for him to hit the ball. But he kept trying and after a few weeks he began playing imaginary matches with the garage wall.

Bjorn says he "invented" international tournaments between Sweden and the United States. If he hit the ball back against the garage wall five times, he and Sweden won the point. But, if he missed the ball or didn't hit it back five times, the United States won the point.

A few weeks later, Bjorn went to the Sodertalje Tennis Club. He wanted to register in a beginner's class. The teacher told him all the classes were filled. Instead of giving up, Bjorn went home and played more tennis with the garage wall.

Because no one taught him how to hit backhands, and because his racket was too big and heavy to swing with one hand, Bjorn says he started using a two-handed backhand.

After a few more weeks Bjorn went back to the Tennis Club and pestered the teacher so much he found room for him in a class. Bjorn says he practically lived on the tennis courts that summer. He started at seven o'clock every morning and played until his parents came to get him in the evening.

After his lesson, Bjorn says he practiced and then practiced more. He just wanted to practice and play tennis. He practiced hard because his parents taught him never to give up once he started something. Bjorn says his parents told him he didn't have to play tennis. But, if he wanted to be good, he'd have to work at it—hard—everyday.

At first, Bjorn says, he was a clumsy tennis player. He had no timing on his serve and reminded his opponents of a charging bull. But day by day, he got better.

Bjorn Borg will be a power in tennis for many years.

Borg decided that he'd do better playing tennis than staying in school.

Bjorn's last class at school ended at 3:00. After school Bjorn says he'd run to catch a train to Stockholm so he could practice on an indoor court. After a two-hour train ride, Bjorn practiced for two or three hours. Bjorn says his fast tennis game developed while playing on the hardboard floors in gyms. After practice, Bjorn got back on the train and arrived home at 10:00 in the evening.

When Bjorn was ten, he met Percy Rosberg, a World Class tennis player in the 1950's. He was one of Sweden's national tennis coaches. Scouting junior players for the national team, Percy's sharp eyes spotted Bjorn's skillful play. Bjorn's hard work and enthusiasm impressed Percy so much he began teaching and training him immediately.

Bjorn says Percy not only helped him develop his own natural talent, but also recognized and did not try to change his natural gift for tennis.

Percy says Bjorn hit his forehand then the same way he does today—all wrist—like he's playing table tennis. Bjorn learned that while playing table tennis with his father. Bjorn says he liked Percy's teaching methods—criticism, encouragement, and praise. Percy also taught him tournament technique and tactics.

All those lonely train rides and late nights paid off. Bjorn won a school tennis tournament at age 12. Then he won another school tournament and a county medal. In 1970, he won at the Bastad tournament, Sweden's most important competition for young people. By the time he was 14, Bjorn had won every school and junior championship in Sweden.

There wasn't anymore competition for Bjorn in Sweden. So, sponsored by the Swedish Tennis Federation, he traveled to an international junior tournament in Berlin, Germany. He won that tournament, defeating players three years older. The young teen went on to win junior tournaments in Barcelona, Spain, Milan, Italy, and at the Orange Bowl in Miami, Florida.

Because Bjorn spent so much time traveling and playing tennis, his school work suffered. As a ninth grader at Blombacka School, Bjorn experienced several problems. Teachers complained about his absences and missing homework. Bjorn says his biology and geography teacher told him his homework was never correct and he didn't know anything. Bjorn replied that he didn't need to study geography in school because he traveled and experienced geography firsthand.

When he didn't know the right answers, Bjorn says some teachers tried to embarrass him by asking more questions. Finally, he told the teachers it wasn't doing anyone any good to keep asking him questions because he didn't know anything anyway.

Bjorn discussed these problems with his parents. He told them he was wasting his time, sitting in a classroom between eight and three. He couldn't sit still for an hour, hearing teachers make fun of him. Bjorn said he hated school, wasn't learning anything, and wanted to quit.

All he really wanted to do, Bjorn says, was play tennis. If his parents let him quit school he promised to give himself five years to make one million dollars as a tennis player. If he didn't reach that goal, he promised to quit tennis and try something new.

A few days later Bjorn and his parents met with the school's headmaster and Bjorn's teachers. The headmaster said Bjorn couldn't quit school before finishing the ninth grade. But one teacher argued it would hurt Bjorn to force him to stay in school. The teacher said it would be best for Bjorn to leave school because he already knew what he wanted to do. He had already chosen his profession—playing tennis.

Finally, after several discussions, Bjorn's parents and the headmaster gave him permission to leave school. Bjorn said he hoped to make enough money so he'd never have to go back to school and be made fun of again.

After leaving school, Bjorn traveled to the Swedish Tennis Federation's training camp on the Riviera. There Lennart Bergelin, a Wimbledon quarterfinalist and former Davis Cup player, worked on Bjorn's game.

Bjorn's tennis skills sharpened after several lessons and many, many hours of practice. The hard work paid off quickly. When he was only 15, Bjorn qualified for Sweden's Davis Cup team! Bjorn earned his position by defeating Jan-Erik Lundquist 6-3, 6-2 in the Madrid Grand Prix. Bjorn was called the best junior tennis player in the world.

At 18, Borg was the youngest ever to win the French International Title.

In May 1972, Bjorn became one of the youngest players ever to play in the Davis Cup. In his first match he played Onny Parun, ranked #1 in New Zealand. Bjorn lost the first two sets 4-6, 3-6. But he didn't give up. Playing like a determined professional, he fought back and won the next three sets.

After the match, Bjorn said it didn't matter how far behind he was because in tennis, if you take the last point you always have a chance to win.

Although just a teenager, Bjorn didn't fear older players. In 1973 he defeated such champions as Ken Rosewall, Arthur Ashe, and Ilie Nastase. At 17, Bjorn's ranking rocketed to World Class—the youngest World Class player ever! His 1973 earnings reached $62,500.

That year, John Newcombe, three-time Wimbledon champion and winner of two U.S. Opens, said Bjorn was the best 17-year-old tennis player in the world. "But he was more than that," Newcombe added. Bjorn was the nicest guy Newcombe had ever met. Newcombe went on to say he hoped his son would be just as good a sportsman as Bjorn Borg.

On June 3, 1974, Bjorn's play rewrote tennis history! Defeating Ilie Nastase 6-3, 6-4, 6-2, he won the Italian Open. That made him the youngest player ever to win a major international tennis tournament! "That victory was important," Bjorn says, "because I gained international respect and self-confidence."

In 1976, Borg dreamed of taking his first Wimbledon championship.

Then the terrific teen won another major tournament! He captured the French Open, which many people say is the clay court championship of the world. Bjorn won it the hard way, after losing the first two sets 2-6, 5-7. Refusing to give up, he fought back and won the next three sets 6-0, 6-1, 6-1, to defeat Manuel Orantes. Afterwards Bjorn again claimed a tennis match is never over until the match-point has been won. "Turn defeat into victory," Bjorn says. It's one of his favorite slogans.

Bjorn Borg is the youngest tennis player ever to accomplish so much so quickly—two Wimbledon titles, two French Opens, one World Championship Tennis (WCT) title, one Italian Open, and three United States Professional titles. Playing for the Cleveland Nets of World Team tennis, he was voted Team Tennis Player of the Year in 1977.

At 18 his tennis winnings topped $100,000. At 20 his prize money climbed over $400,000. He earned about half a million more dollars playing in exhibitions, making personal appearances, and giving his name to products. As a 21-year-old, Bjorn earned between one and one-half to two million dollars.

The way Bjorn Borg wins tennis tournaments may seem easy. It's not. He wins because he spends many, many hours practicing and training. Because he spends so much time practicing, Bjorn says he doesn't have time to have close friendships. Because he wants to stay in shape, Bjorn says he doesn't eat chocolates and ice cream.

Bjorn has devoted his life to tennis. Tennis *is* his life, he says, it's in his blood. Bjorn says he'd go mad if he couldn't play tennis. Tennis is all he knows or wants to know.

He practices for at least two hours every day and gets at least 9 hours of sleep every night. Before the 1976 Wimbledon, he practiced just his serves for two hours each day. He worked so hard his stomach muscles tightened and hurt. But his skillful, powerful serves were one of the reasons he won that tournament.

Borg thinks hard before he speaks. He never rushes into anything.

Although Bjorn has won several major tournaments and is one of the best players in the world, he says he still must practice many hours to maintain and improve his skills. Because he practiced so much and played in so many tournaments, Bjorn says he missed growing up like the average youth.

But, Bjorn says, it was his choice. No one forced him to practice. He wanted to practice and practice and give tennis 100 per cent of his energy. Why? Bjorn says he just wanted to be the best tennis player in the world.

Sometimes, Bjorn says, he feels like giving it all up. On some days, he feels so tired he never wants to play tennis again. On other days he says he hates tennis.

"It's tough to be strong mentally," Bjorn says, "even when you're a champion." It's hard to go to sleep early in the evening, get up early in the morning, practice, play in tournaments, pack suitcases, catch airplanes, check into hotels, unpack suitcases, and then practice some more. "To do this, day after day, year after year, is very difficult, very tiring," Bjorn says.

"I've gotten good advice from my friends," Borg says. Here he's with an old friend and fellow tennis pro, Arthur Ashe.

Bjorn Borg's goal was to become a millionaire by age 21.

What do the people on the other side of the net say about Bjorn? Vitas Gerulaitis, who lost to Bjorn in a thrilling match at the 1977 Wimbledon, says Bjorn is very friendly. He will do anything for you. He's considerate, polite. He'll talk to anyone. "Bjorn is a great worker," Vitas adds, "a very hard worker." He's the best at what he does. He doesn't have time for other things.

Roscoe Tanner, a World Class player, says he likes Bjorn Borg. He's a very good guy. "To be #1," Roscoe says, "You have to play well on all surfaces." He says Bjorn does just that.

Other players say Bjorn plays tennis now like it will be played in the future. He hits every shot hard, about six feet over the net. It lands six feet inside the baseline because he puts so much topspin on the ball.

Jack Kramer, a Wimbledon winner and U.S. Open champion, says Bjorn's rackets are strung so tight that if the average player used one for any length of time, his or her arm would fall off. Bjorn's rackets are strung at 80 pounds tension. Some stringers say it's almost impossible to string a racket so tight.

Many players use the same racket for several weeks or longer. Bjorn breaks between 10 and 15 every week. When he hits the ball, the "ping" sounds like a ray-gun shooting in a science fiction movie. When Bjorn breaks a string, it sounds like a gunshot!

"Bjorn is an international champion," Jack Kramer says, "because he can change his stroke to meet any surface." Bjorn grew up playing on clay, so he's tough to beat on slow surfaces. But he's done well on fast surfaces, such as Wimbledon's slick grass.

Bjorn is a fast mover on the tennis court, other players say. He knows what's coming, so during rallies it's hard to knock outright winners past him.

The weakest part of Bjorn's game, many players say, is his volley, especially his backhand. His two-fisted style limits his reach and makes it hard for him to hit balls deep, especially on low volleys.

Bjorn's passing shots are superb, many players say. The best way to beat Bjorn, his opponents claim, is to take command of the net. To beat him, you must mix speed and spin cleverly. Players defeat Bjorn by stroking soft balls which prevent him from finding a groove. Opponents know they can't win once Bjorn establishes a rhythm.

Guillermo Vilas, winner of the 1977 U.S. Open, says Bjorn plays with a very strong mind. "Bjorn won Wimbledon," Guillermo says, "because he played the strongest mental game."

Lennart Bergelin, Bjorn's coach, says Bjorn may appear calm on the surface, but underneath there is fire. Bjorn is mentally tough.

What do people who watch Bjorn say about him? Many newspapers and magazines call him a playboy. Bjorn says many untrue stories have been printed about him. It bothers him when people write he's a playboy. Bjorn says he's never been a playboy. That he's the same guy he was when he was a youngster in school, quiet and shy.

Girls, Bjorn says, turn him off and scare him when they scream and chase him. He says he doesn't have any groupies and doesn't want to be an idolized superstar. Bjorn says he has just one girl friend—Mariana Simionescu, a World Class player from Rumania and teammate on the Cleveland Nets. Bjorn and Mariana became engaged on November 4, 1976.

Borg enjoys relaxing and taking his mind off tennis.

Though Borg is very cool about championship tennis, he's really an enthusiastic person.

Bjorn has other problems with reporters. In 1977 he said he didn't play in the Davis Cup for Sweden because he feared and disliked the Swedish press. He said they wrote untrue articles about his private life, his parents, his coach, and Mariana. The Swedish people read those articles, Bjorn says, and believed them. This disappointed him very much.

Chatting with his coach.

But, despite these problems, Bjorn says he's never been happier. He enjoys tennis and is in love with Mariana. "It's important to be happy off the court," Bjorn says. "Happiness helps your tennis game."

Does Bjorn Borg have any tips for young tennis players? He says young people, especially beginners, should never worry about the player on the other side of the net. "Don't get excited or nervous," Bjorn says. "Just concentrate on hitting the ball. All you have to do is make sure you win the next point."

"One of the most important ideas young tennis players must understand," Bjorn says, "is never give up—no matter how far down you are!"

"Make your tennis stroke as simple as possible," Bjorn says. To win a point, you just have to hit the ball over the net one more time than your opponent.

"A player who can't control emotions on the court will never be a great tennis player," Bjorn adds. When he began playing tennis, Bjorn admits he had a terrible temper. He threw rackets and broke several. During practice matches with friends, Bjorn says he sometimes cheated because he wanted to win so badly. This embarrassed and disappointed his parents. His parents told him his tennis would never improve if he behaved badly on the court. Bjorn says he finally realized he would win more matches if he controlled his temper.

Sure, Bjorn still gets upset during matches. But he doesn't want to show his opponents how he feels. Sometimes he feels like throwing his racket. But he holds back and controls his emotions.

"Young people," Bjorn explains, "should understand the Swedish slogan, 'ice in your stomach.' It means keep cool, calm, concentrated. You should never show, by the slightest flicker of an eyelid, that your opponent is making an impression on you."

Bjorn encourages all young players to play in tough tournaments against skillful players. The sooner young people get to know the best players, both as people and players, the greater their chances to defeat them.

The World Class players are ordinary people, according to Bjorn. If you play with them, they usually give you advice and tips, eat lunch and dinner with you, and strengthen your self-confidence. Bjorn says Arthur Ashe helped him by advising him never to worry about who was on the other side of the net.

Above all, Bjorn believes you can't play good tennis unless you train properly—at least two hours of hitting tennis balls every day of the year, about nine hours of sleep every night. Eating good food is very important too, Bjorn says. The 5' 10", 150-pounder usually eats steak and vegetables and drinks mineral water every day. Sometimes, he allows himself the luxury of eating fish—sole is one of his favorites.

"In addition you will never win a match, unless you take some risks," Borg claims. "For example, you must hit some daring stop-balls once in a while. Don't let your opponent know what to expect. If he or she is expecting a topspin lob, hit the ball with a chop shot. Before you can ever hope to win, you must convince yourself you can beat your opponent. You must never be afraid of losing."

After years of practice, Bjorn Borg has become one of the best and richest players in professional tennis.

"If you lose a point, a game, a set, a match, or a tournament," Bjorn says, "you must forget all about it immediately. Look forward to the next point, game, set, match, and tournament."

"To keep on winning," Bjorn explains, "you must maintain a strong will and fighting spirit. You must stay mentally fit. You must concentrate."

When Bjorn Borg isn't playing tennis, what kind of person is he? His private life is quiet and simple. He's a peaceful young man, doesn't get upset easily, and doesn't complain. Many people say Bjorn is level-headed and is hardly ever sad or depressed.

Off the tennis court, Bjorn walks casually, with a rocking, side-to-side motion like Charlie Chaplin did in his films. When people ask him for his autograph, he scrawls a barely readable BB. When he speaks English, he talks carefully, slowly, and softly.

Bjorn loves his parents. When he was 17 he gave them a summer home. Because they always wanted to run their own business, he bought them a grocery store. Now his parents live in Monte Carlo, operating their own store—The Bjorn Borg Sports Shop.

Like many young people, Bjorn enjoys wearing jeans, T-shirts, and tennis or gym shoes. "Gold chokers and turquoise beads are fun to wear," he adds.

Discipline and planning keep Borg on top. Here he marks his practice
calendar.

Throughout the world, Bjorn travels with a dark chocolate-colored stuffed bunny. He says it's his "Good Luck Bunny." He never travels without his portable tape recorder and at least seventy tapes. His favorite recordings are by Elvis Presley. Shirley Bassey, the Beatles, and Cat Stevens are some of his other favorites.

Going to the beach, sunbathing, and swimming are some of the ways Bjorn spends his free time. He also enjoys reading comic strips and comic books. He says Donald Duck, featuring Goofy and Pluto, amuses him.

But, Bjorn says, his favorite pastime is just relaxing—resting and not doing anything.

Because he's earning a living from his favorite hobby, Bjorn says he's having the greatest fun there is!

What's in Bjorn Borg's future? Many players, reporters, and fans say he will dominate tennis until 1990. Bjorn says he wants to keep on playing and winning as long as he can. "It feels good to win," he says. And he wants that very nice feeling of winning many more times in the future.

Borg and his fiancee, Mariana after his Wimbledon victory.

Bjorn's style is so cool, the Swedes say he has "ice in his stomach."

Because Bjorn plays so hard, so all-out, and with such explosive energy, many people say he must be careful not to burn himself out. They say he must avoid playing so much he becomes stale or over-tennised. During the quarterfinals of the 1977 U.S. Open, he defaulted because of a shoulder injury. But, after resting, he recovered quickly and three weeks later won $35,000 and the men's singles title at the World Invitational Classic by defeating Roscoe Tanner.

His goal, Bjorn said, was to win Wimbledon three times and be seeded #1—the best tennis player in the world.

On Saturday, July 8, 1978, the 22-year-old Swede achieved his goals. Belting bullet-like serves (5 aces) and topspin returns, Bjorn easily defeated Jimmy Connors, 6-2, 6-2, 6-3, in only 1 hour and 48 minutes. The victory was his third at Wimbledon and equaled the record set by Fred Perry, the British star who won there in 1934, 1935, and 1936. Bjorn was truly the best tennis player in the world!

When he retires from playing tournament tennis, Bjorn says he wants to teach at tennis camps and clinics. He says he doesn't want to sit in a chair by the pool and watch the water. Acting in movies also interests him. He says he'd like to play an emotional role, something with feelings, like a soldier returning home from war.

Whatever he does, Bjorn Borg will always be a champion, many players, reporters and fans say, because he has the heart and the cool to pull it off.

GLOSSARY

angle shot a ball hit at an angle

backcourt an eighteen foot area behind the service line

backhand a stroke made with the racket with the back of the hand facing outward and the arm moving forward

baseline the rear boundary line at each end of the court

chop shot a short downward hit of the ball with a racket giving the ball backspin

Davis Cup an international tennis tournament played every year

forehand a stroke made with the racket with the palm of the hand turned in the direction in which the ball is being shot

game a unit of scoring; four points equal a game

groove a rhythm or pattern of play in which a player can do best

lob a stroke that sends the ball in a high arc over the opponent's head, and down near the back of the court

match a competition between players or teams which ends when one side wins the most of a specific number of games

match point the last point needed to win a match

point a unit of scoring made by a player when an opponent fails to make a good return

quarterfinalist a competitor in the quarterfinals of tournament play, where the number of players has been reduced from eight to four

rallies a number of plays with the ball shot back and forth across the net until a player fails to return it and the other side scores a point

seeded ranked; based on skill and ability

serving the act of putting a ball into play

set a unit of scoring where six games have been won with a lead score of two games, or when play continues until a two point lead is made by one player or team

shot the act of propelling or moving a ball forward

spin the act of striking a ball slightly or off center, so that it rotates; and bounces or rebounds at an unusual angle

92
BOR

Hahn, James.

Bjorn Borg, the
coolest ace.